Moon Child

A relaxing, empowering journey through poetry and colouring

By Freya O'Brien

Copyright (c) 2023 by Freya O'Brien

All rights reserved. No part of this publication may be reproduced, distributed or transmitted in any form or by any means, including photocopying, recording, or other electronic or mechanical methods, without prior written permission from the publisher, except in the case of brief quotations embodied in critical reviews and other non-commercial uses permitted by copyright law.

First Printing, 2023

ISBN-13: 978-1-7397933-8-8

I hope that by the end of this book, you feel as vibrant as your colouring pages.

All my love,
Freya

Contents

- Relax — 5
- Dream — 25
- Love & Empower — 55

The birds flutter and sing
to the delicate tune
of a silent piano,
as the sun rises
over the sleepy hills
and whispers hello.

Sleepy soft clouds float
across the tender sky,
as emerald blades of grass
rustle in the breeze.

A mother and daughter
play in the field,
laughing at the grass stains
on their knees.

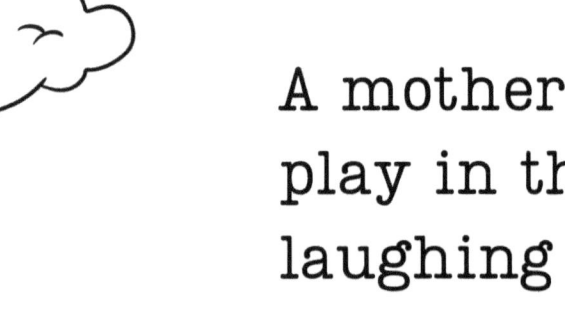

The willows whisper
as the wind caresses
her skin,
and the natural world
tries to soothe
the struggles she faces
within.

The smell of pine cones
and wet soil fills her lungs.
The longer she stays
in the forest,
the harder going home
becomes.

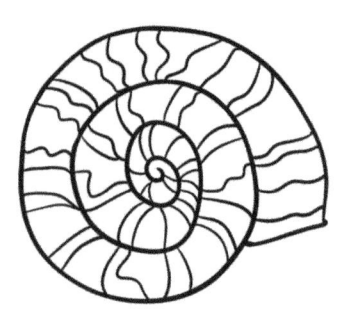 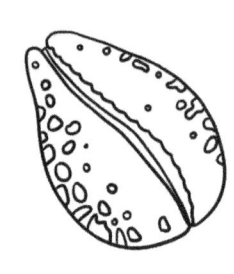  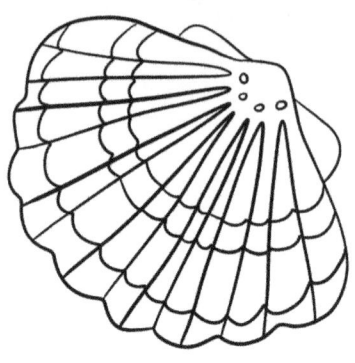

As the waves crash,
and sand falls
through my toes;
the water caresses
my skin,
and carries away
my woes.

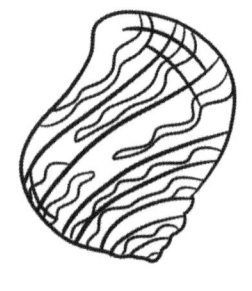 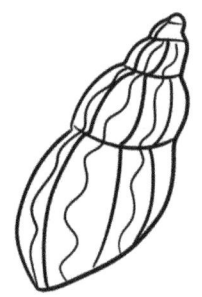

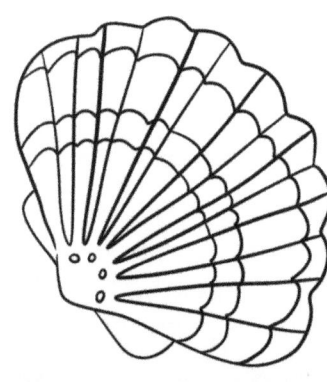  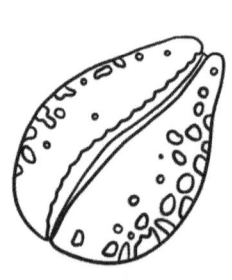 

Wellies echo along
the rain drenched cobblestone.
The pitter patter of rainfall
makes us feel less alone.

The sun dances
with the white horses
galloping across the sea bed.
They crash and melt
into the shoreline,
as birds fly overhead.

A girl picks up sea shells,
and hears the waves
in her ears,
as she wishes for adventure
in the ocean she reveres.

The sun drenched clouds
say goodbye,
as twilight
takes them away.

Serenity speaks through
the whispers of raindrops,
the glimmer of rainbows,
and the rustle of leaves;
calming our busy minds
as we finally stop
and listen.

A mermaid's song echoes
in the glistening blue ocean,
to the furthest corners
of the deep.
As her fish friends
are rocked by the tide,
they gently fall asleep.

If I could fly,
I would spend eternity
running my fingertips
through clouds;
following the sun
as it colours the sky.

Her sapphire eyes
reflect the serene sea,
as she eagerly awaits her ship.

She cannot wait to experience the
magic and wonder
beyond her shores.

She bathed in moonlight,
as her heart burns
for the stars.

Fairies dance across puddles,
to the symphony
of children's laughter,
as they play together
in the rain.

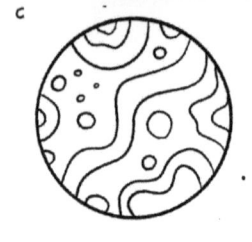

Everyone adores the sun
and her rays,
brightening the world
and giving us days.

But who adores the
moon queen and her light,
guiding the way
for all at night.

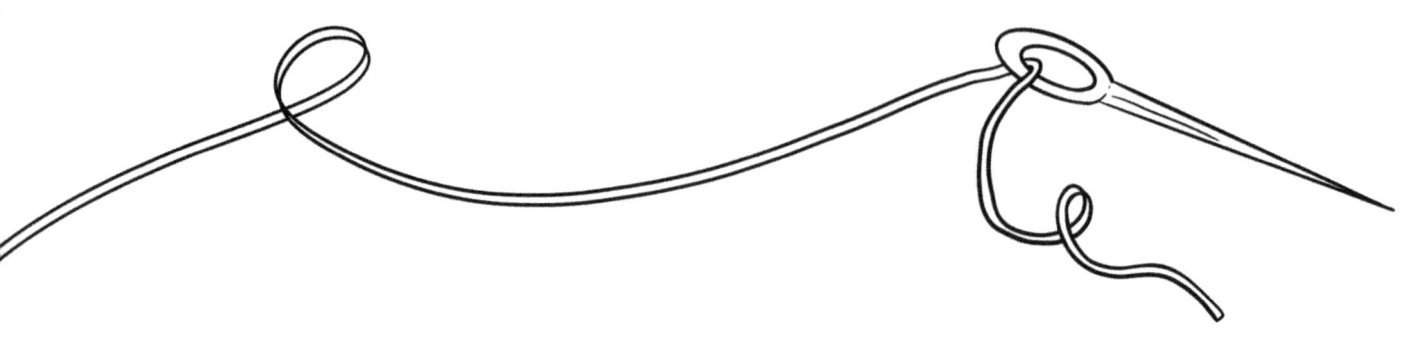

She sits on the moon,
her eyes are hopeful
and bright.
As she sews stars
into the sky,
for all to admire at night.

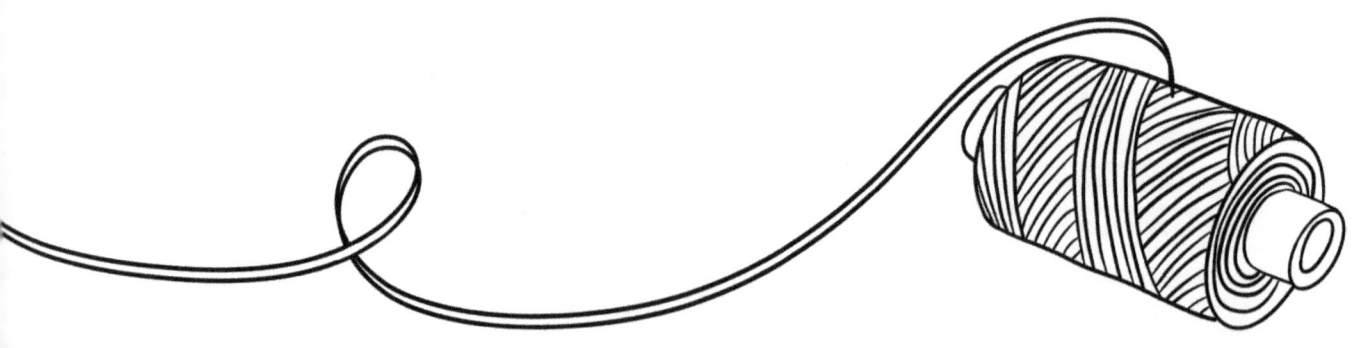

Sweet flowers blooming,
fairies dancing,
colours radiant,
in children's dreams.

The night sky hums with melodies and moonbeams, as I lie here wishing to swim amidst the stars.

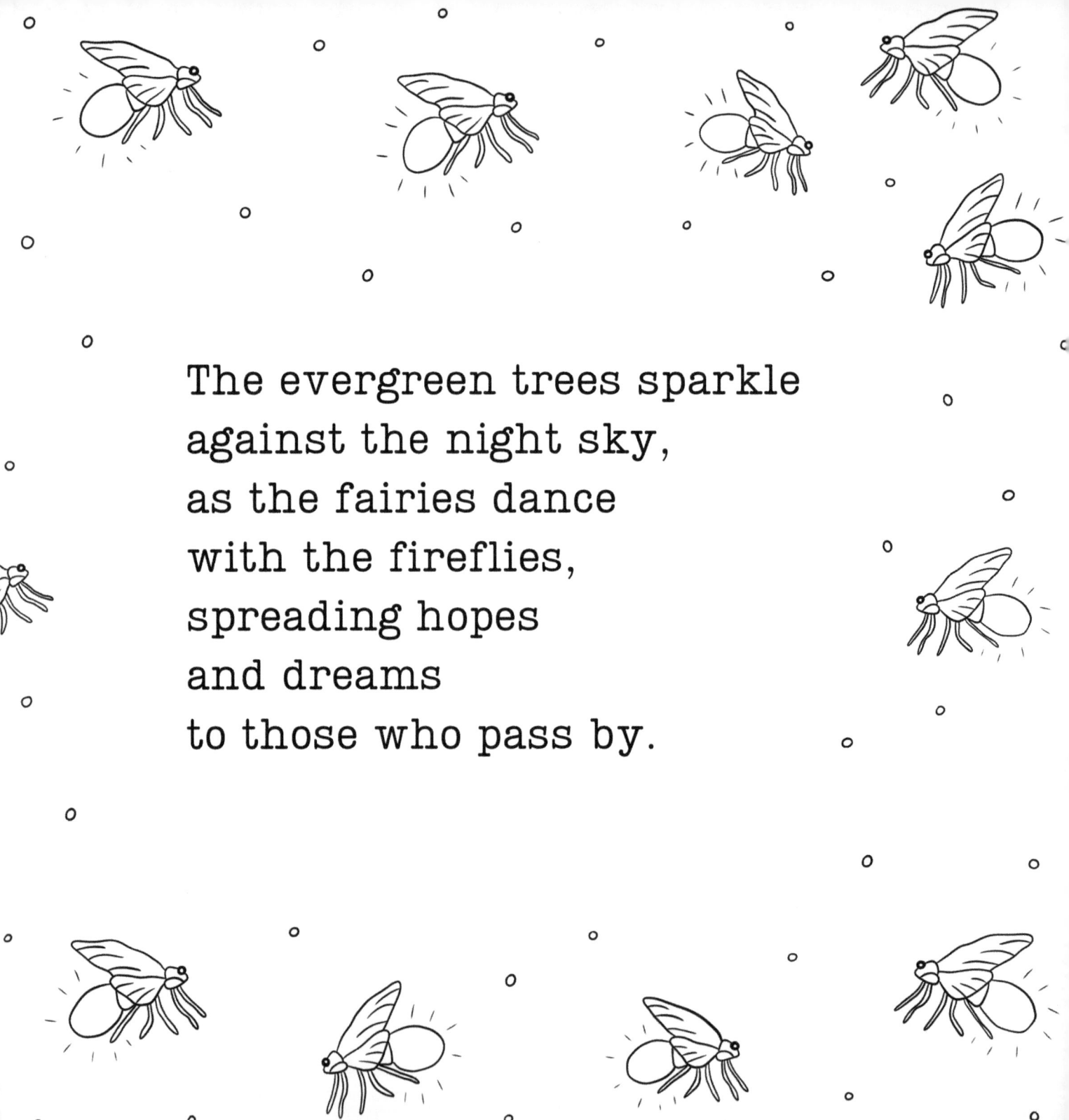

The evergreen trees sparkle
against the night sky,
as the fairies dance
with the fireflies,
spreading hopes
and dreams
to those who pass by.

Her soft green eyes
mirror galaxies,
with their flecks of gold.
Her hair dances in the wind
as it whispers
"look and behold".

As the moon sings
a lullaby for her children,
iridescent sapphire waves
dance along the
sleeping shore.

The owls sing from
tree hollows,
as the sun rests
her weary head.
Alerting the night sky
and all her creatures,
it's their time
to play instead.

My dear,
you are like a kintsugi vase.
Your healing journey
from a place of brokenness,
is beautiful to behold.

My mind is a temple.
Only thoughts forged
from love and respect
will be welcome to stay.

Her beauty and spirit
has been forged from
life's cruel hands,
as she keeps on
optimistically fighting
to live out
her dreams and plans.

Moon child,
the night sky whispers
your name,
as your mind reflects
the stars.

As days become darker,
and the night sky dances
for longer,
a symphony of stars
and planets
whisper to those who listen:

Look up summer child,
for you are not lost
in darkness
but embraced by it.

My dear,
like a sunflower
you will always find
the light.

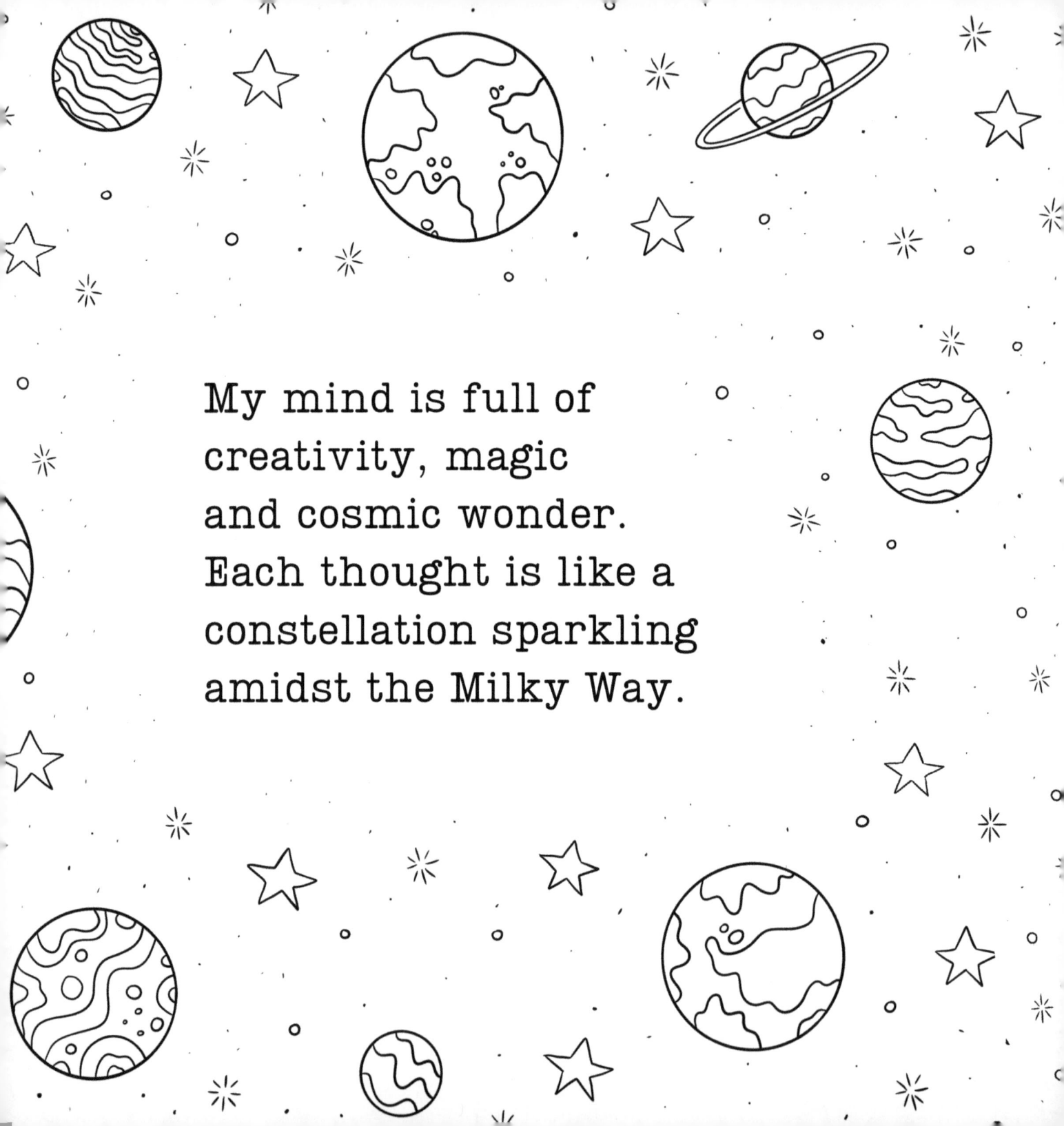

My mind is full of creativity, magic and cosmic wonder. Each thought is like a constellation sparkling amidst the Milky Way.

I am like a rose with its thorns, beautiful and powerful.

I carry my dreams
with me,
like a jar of fireflies
illuminating the way.

You can forge
the life you want
with your will of fire.
Don't let anyone
dull your flames.

You are bold, beautiful,
and hold magic
in your hands.
For if you can dream it,
you can make it.
So go forge your wonderland!

Even without rainbows,
wishing stars and
fairy godmothers,
nothing is impossible.
You can find the magic
you need in your heart,
where it's always been.

You smiled at me,
and suddenly I was
a sapphire sky,
enveloped by the moon
and stars.

You are the moon to my tides,
Pulling me into your orbit.

Freya O'Brien is an English poet and illustrator who channels her heart through her pen. She creates poems and illustrations based on her personal life, thoughts and emotions.

Freya uses a pen and paper as an outlet on the darkest of days, to celebrate life, and connect with those who may be able to relate.

Find Freya online at:

- @by_freyaobrien on Instagram
- www.freya-obrien.com

Share your colouring with the hashtag #moonchildcolouring for a chance to be featured on Freya's social media.

More books by Freya O'Brien

If MOON CHILD felt like a friend,
you may find comfort in these pages too…

If you've ever navigated broken homes, toxic love, or the long path of emotional healing, LONELY LINES is a companion for the dark, quiet hours — and a gentle light for what comes after.

If you've felt the weight of grief, illness, or a world that feels unbearably heavy, HOLLOW BONES will walk beside you, offering space to grieve, reflect, and gently rebuild.

Available from Amazon, Freya's website, and other booksellers.

www.ingramcontent.com/pod-product-compliance
Lightning Source LLC
Chambersburg PA
CBHW042036100526
44587CB00030B/4443